With thanks to the veterinary surgeon Kamiel Warnants of De Brem animal clinic

For Roos and Fien

First published in Belgium and the Netherlands by Clavis Uitgeverij, 2010
Copyright © 2010, Clavis Uitgeverij

English translation from the Dutch by Clavis Publishing Inc. New York
Copyright © 2019 for the English language edition: Clavis Publishing Inc. New York

Visit us on the Web at www.clavis-publishing.com

Veterinarians and What They Do written and illustrated by Liesbet Slegers
Original title: *De dierenarts*
Translated from the Dutch by Clavis Publishing

ISBN 978-1-60537-495-6

This book was printed in November 2020 at Nikara,
M. R. Štefánika 858/25, 963 01 Krupina, Slovakia.

First Edition
10 9 8 7 6 5 4 3 2

Veterinarians
and What They Do
Liesbet Slegers

Clavis

NEW YORK

When you get a new pet, you will take it to visit the veterinarian.

A vet is a doctor for animals.

She will tell you what to do to keep your pet healthy.

What does your pet need to eat?

Where does it like to sleep? Your vet knows all about it.

The vet will also help you if your pet is sick.

She explains what you need to do to make it better.

surgical mask

Vets work with animals all day, so they wear comfortable clothes.
For an operation she might wear: a long green apron, a surgical mask,
a paper hat, and white gloves.
These clothes help keep things clean.

paper hat

gloves

long apron

place to relax

The vet examines the animal with a stethoscope and a thermometer.

Sometimes she takes a photograph of a little paw, to see if it is broken.

Maybe the animal needs an injection or other medicines.

If the animal needs an operation the big lamp helps the vet see.

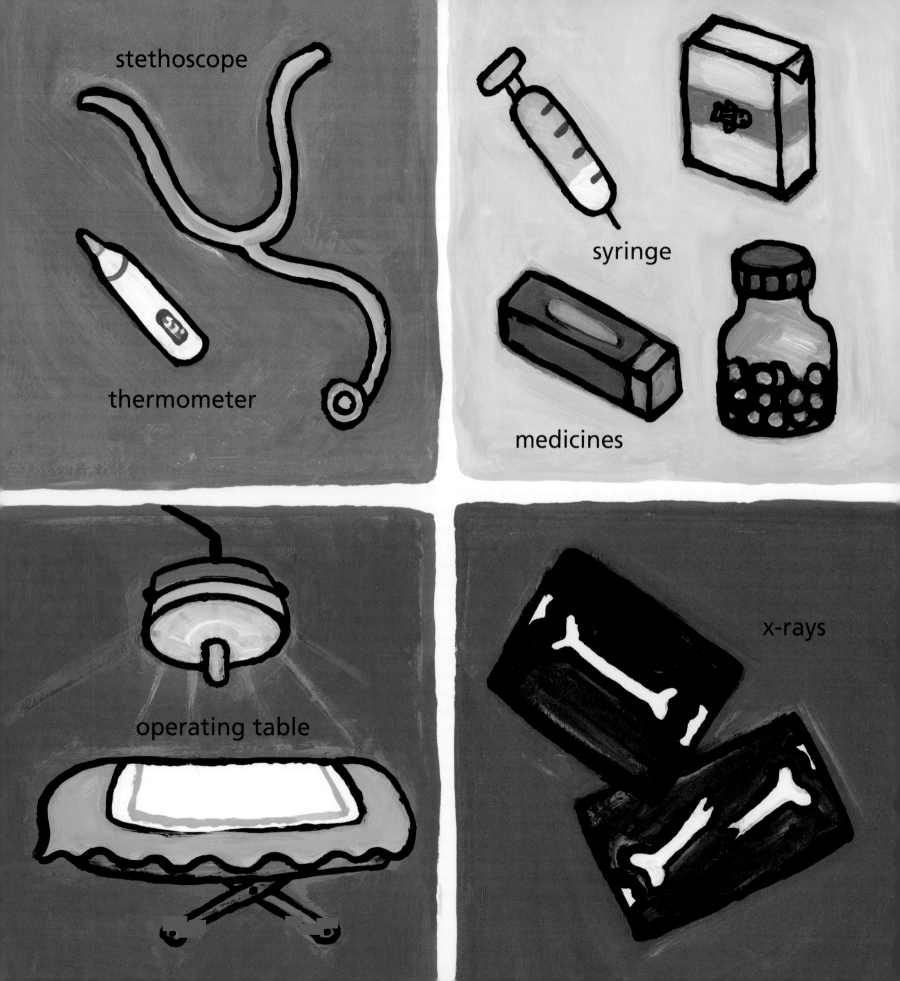

stethoscope

thermometer

syringe

medicines

operating table

x-rays

"Hi, Doctor. Can you take a look at my puppy?

He seems tired and doesn't want to eat his food."

"Maybe he has a stomachache," the vet says.

"Come with me. Let's put him on the table

so I can take a look at him."

The vet examines the puppy.

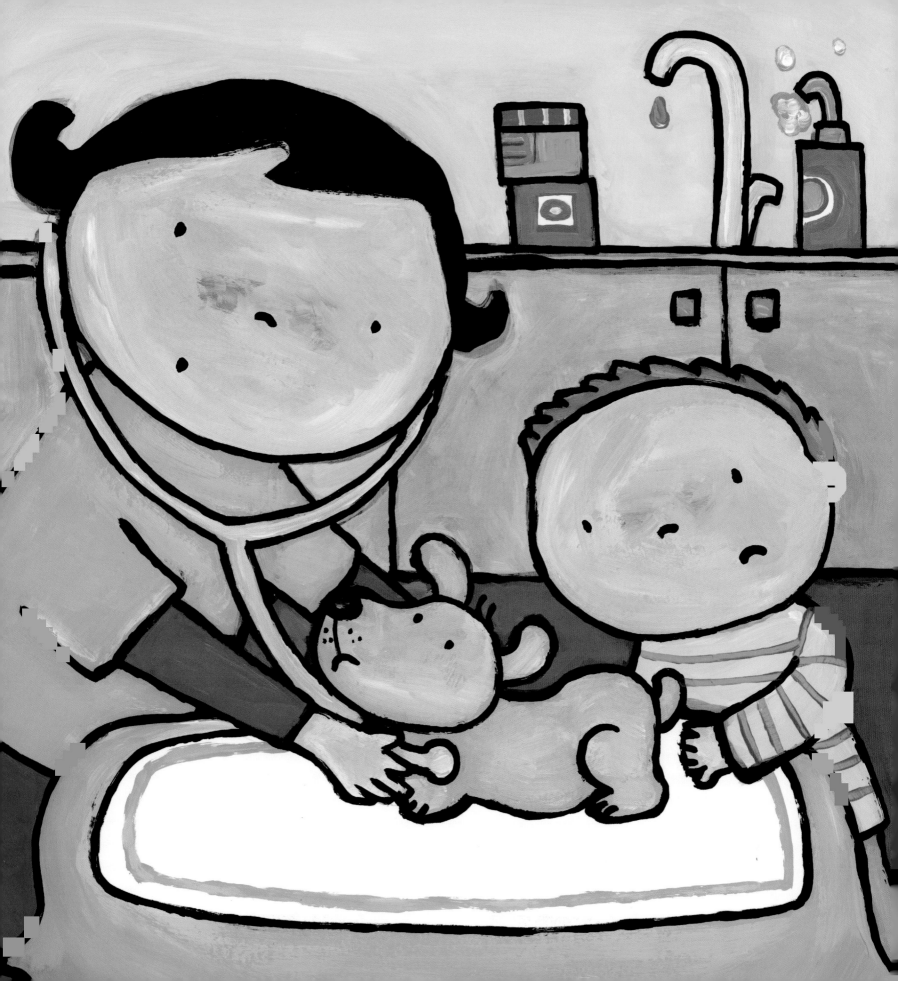

"I will take an x-ray of his belly," she says,

"to see what is wrong and how I can help him."

"Will it hurt?" the boy wants to know.

"Oh, no. He won't feel a thing," the vet promises.

She brings the little dog into a special room.

The vet's assistant holds the dog tight

so he won't move when the photograph is being taken.

"All right!" the vet says. "What a good dog."

"Aha, look at that," the vet says to the boy.

"Do you see that little ball on the x-ray?

Your puppy has a stomachache

because he swallowed a little toy ball."

"What is going to happen now?" the boy wants to know.

"With an operation I can remove the little ball from his stomach.

After that, your puppy will soon be well again."

First the dog is put to sleep with an injection.

He gets some air and medicine through a small tube so he can breathe and stay asleep.

Maybe he is dreaming of a delicious bone, or a run in the park!

The vet operates to remove the little toy ball from his belly.

There it is!

Now the little dog will rest in a cage.

There are other animals resting too. Each one has their own spot.

They can all slowly wake up from their operations.

It may take a few days before they can go back home.

Finally, the puppy can go home.

He is all better.

"Thank you, doctor!" the boy says. "I can't wait to play with him!"

"But be careful with those little balls, won't you?" the vet warns him.

The little boy nods and smiles. The vet gives the puppy

a treat because he has been such a good dog.

Just then, the vet gets an urgent call.

A girl tried to jump with her pony over a fence,

but the animal didn't jump high enough!

It bumped its hind legs into the fence,

and now it is hurt.

Luckily, the girl didn't fall from her pony.

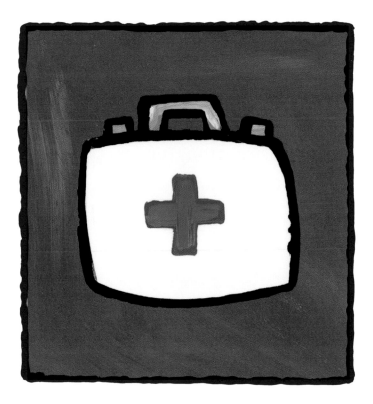

The vet hurries to the meadow. She examines the pony and wraps a bandage around his two hind legs.

"There you are," the vet says. "Leave this bandage on his legs, and make sure he rests. He will be better soon."

"I hope so," the girl says, worried. "Thank you, Doctor!"

A week later the vet pays another visit to the pony and the girl.

The animal is all better.

The girl is very happy. She painted the vet

a picture. "Thank you!" the doctor says.

"I will hang it on the wall of my animal clinic."

Neigh! the pony whinnies happily.

How nice it is to be able to help animals every day.

If you like animals, you might also

want to study to be a vet when you grow up . . .